QED Start Reading AND LISTENING

Mighty Machines

Chris Oxlade

2

QED Publishing

Copyright © QED Publishing 2005

First published in the UK in 2005 by
QED Publishing
A Quarto Group company
226 City Road
London EC1V 2TT
www.qed-publishing.co.uk

A Catalogue record for this book is available from the British Library.

ISBN 1 84538 435 0

Written by Chris Oxlade
Designed by Melissa Alaverdy
Editor Hannah Ray
Picture Researcher Nic Dean

Series Consultant Anne Faundez
Publisher Steve Evans
Creative Director Louise Morley
Editorial Manager Jean Coppendale

Printed and bound in China

Picture credits

Key: t = top, b = bottom, m = middle, l = left, r = right

Aviation Picture Library/Austin J. Brown 13b, 20t /**Corbis**/Lester Lefkowitz 4, /Walter
Hodges 9, 22m, /Lowell Georgia 10, 19b, /Christie & Cole 11, /Matthew Polak 12, 20b,
/George Hall 13/**Freightliner LLC**/Western Star Trucks 8, 19t, 22tl/**Getty Images**/Jimmy
Lee 15, 21b, 22t, 22br/**Liebherr**/courtesy of Liebherr Mining Equipment Co. front cover, 5,
18t/courtesy of Liebherr, manufacturer of the worlds largest range of mobile cranes title
page, 6, 7, 18b/**NASA**/16, 17, 21t, 22b.

Contents

Dumper

driver's cab

body

wheel

4

This mighty machine is a dumper.

It carries earth, rubble and rock.

The dumper's body tips up to dump its load of earth.

This is the biggest dumper in the world.
It could carry a whole house!

Crane

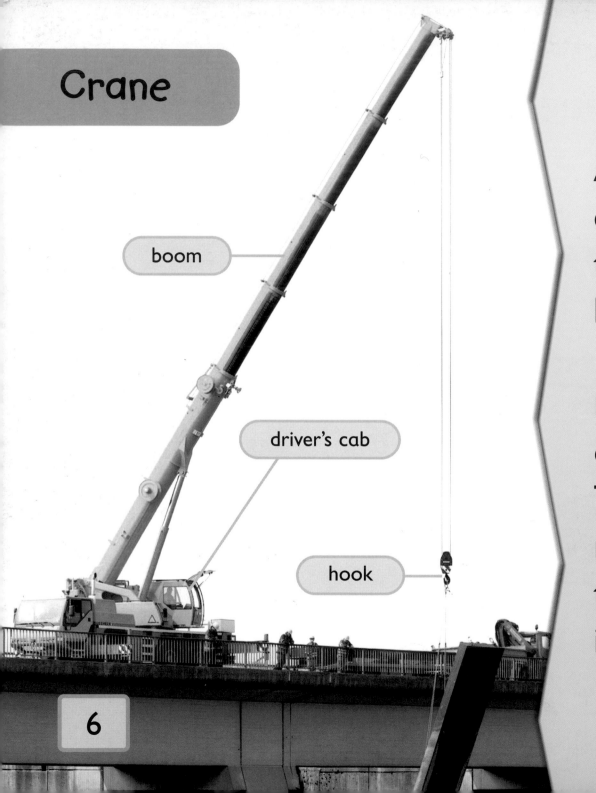

boom

driver's cab

hook

A crane is a machine that lifts heavy things.

Its long arm is called a boom. The boom reaches more than 50 metres into the air.

When the crane has finished a job, the boom folds away. Then the crane drives off to do another job.

Truck

tractor

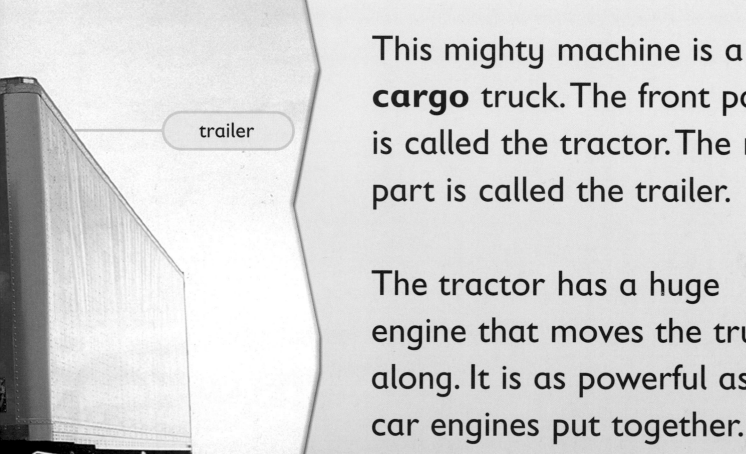

trailer

This mighty machine is a **cargo** truck. The front part is called the tractor. The rear part is called the trailer.

The tractor has a huge engine that moves the truck along. It is as powerful as ten car engines put together.

The trailer carries the cargo.

Digger

arm

track

bucket

10

A digger digs holes on a building site. It has metal tracks to help it to move over the muddy ground.

The driver pulls and pushes **levers** to move the digger's arm and bucket.

The bucket scoops up earth and moves it from one place to another.

11

Airliner

wings

cockpit

This mighty airliner flies through the air. Inside are seats for hundreds of passengers.

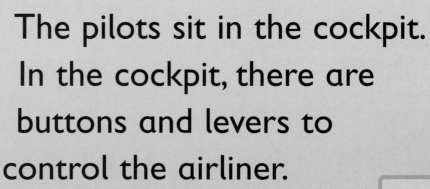

An airliner's wings keep it up in the air, while four huge jet engines push the airliner along.

The pilots sit in the cockpit. In the cockpit, there are buttons and levers to control the airliner.

13

Helicopter

A helicopter is another kind of flying machine.

On the top is a huge **rotor** with lots of thin **blades**. When the rotor spins round, it lifts the helicopter into the air.

This giant helicopter is rescuing a person from the sea.

rotor

blade

15

Space shuttle

booster rocket

shuttle

main engine

booster engine

This mighty machine is a space shuttle.

The space shuttle has its own rocket engines.

There are also two booster rockets. When the engines fire, the shuttle lifts off with a giant roar.

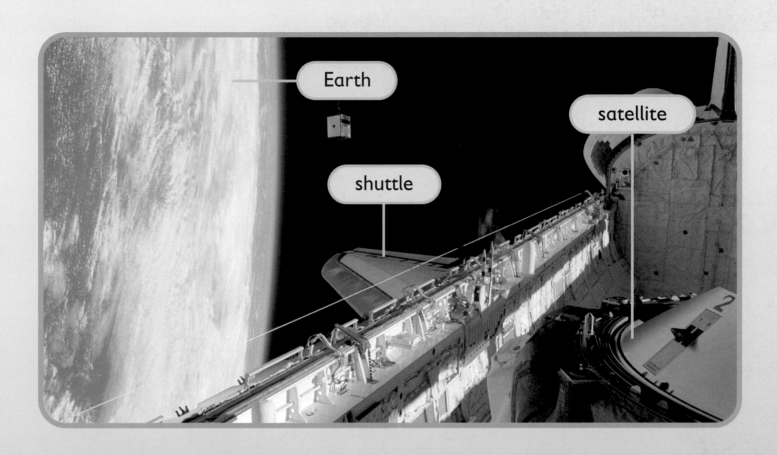

Earth

satellite

shuttle

This shuttle has reached space.
It is launching a **satellite**. Satellites
do many different jobs, such as
sending information and watching
the weather.

What do you think?

How does a dumper empty out its load?

What happens to the boom after the crane has finished its job?

What is the front part of a cargo truck called? What about the rear part?

Why does a digger have metal tracks? How does the driver make a digger's bucket move?

19

Can you remember
where the pilots sit
in an airliner?

What keeps an airliner
up in the air?

Where do shuttles travel to? What pushes a shuttle into space?

What part of a helicopter lifts it into the air?

Blade – a long, flat piece of metal which is part of the rotor.

Cargo – goods carried from place to place by a truck, plane or ship.

Lever – a stick that tilts backwards and forwards or from side to side.

Rotor – the part of a machine that spins round.

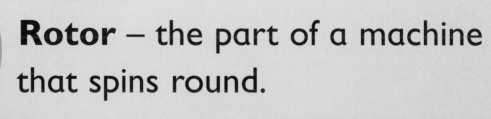

Satellite – a machine in space that moves around the Earth.

Index

23

Parents' and teachers' notes

- Explain to your child that this book is non-fiction (i.e. it gives facts and information rather than telling a story). Point out the contents page, the glossary and the index.

- Explain that the contents page is a list of what is in the book, that the glossary explains difficult words and that the index tells us which page to look at to find specific information.

- Explain to your child that a machine is something that does a job for us and makes our lives easier in some way. Look around your home or school to find examples of machines.

- Explain that the machines in this book are big and complicated, but that there are many simple machines, such as scissors and tin openers, that help us to cut, open, pull and lift.

- Look through the book, discussing each picture as you go. Read the labels out loud. What else could be labelled (wheels, doors, driver, etc.)?

- Point out that each machine in this book needs one or more powerful engines to make it work. Discuss the fact that all these engines use fuel, just like the engine of a car.

- Discuss the people who work the machines (such as truck drivers and pilots). Talk about the skills that each job requires. Which of the machines would your child most like to operate?

- Talk to your child about where dumper trucks, diggers and cranes work (for example, quarries, open-cast mines and building sites). Where might you find each of the other mighty machines?

- Look at pages 8–9 and talk to your child about goods that are carried in trucks. Discuss the fact that everything we buy in the shops arrived there by truck.

- If your child has ever been on an airliner, discuss the flight with him/her. Can your child remember the different parts of an airliner?